SHIPWRECK AROUND ST DAVID'S

by

Tom Bennett

Contents

Page

Happy Fish

A finely carved figurehead found floating in Solva harbour. The author is of the opinion that it belonged to either the schooner VICTORIA lost in 1846 or to the paddle steamer QUEEN lost near Skomer a few years before.

First Published in 1994 by Happy Fish, Holmws, Newport, Dyfed, SA42 0UF.

Page layout by Design 29, Dinas, Dyfed.

Printed in Wales by D.Brown & Sons Ltd, Cowbridge and Bridgend, Glamorgan.

British Library Cataloguing in Publication Data.
A catalogue record of this book is available from the British Library.

Bennett, Tom, 1947-
Shipwrecks around St David's.
1. Shipwrecks- Wales- History
1. Title

ISBN 0 9512114 5 5

Shipwrecks before 1800 - Early Wrecks & Wreckers

Throughout the centuries there have been countless wrecks around the Welsh coastline. Some areas of the coast have an abundance because of the heavy sea traffic or because of greater inherent dangers, the region around St David's is one such area. Records of ship losses before the nineteenth century are sparce and difficult to trace. However, we know that Whitesands was an important landing place for early trade between Ireland and Wales. Saint Patrick himself is said to have sailed to Ireland from Whitesands. The monastic harbour at Porthclais is where the patron Saint of Wales, Saint David, is reported to have been babtised. There is evidence of early human activity in the megalithic tombs at St David's Head, Carn Llidi and the obviously important settlement at Clegyr Boia.

Ever since man commenced his seafaring activities there would have been losses. It is said that Saint David's Cathedral was purposely built in the valley so that it was out of sight of sea rovers. Nevertheless, this did not prevent it from being attacked ten times by Norsemen, and in 1080 Bishop Abraham was slain by them. Both Saint Govan's Chapel and Saint David's Cathedral have a legend relating to a stolen bell. At both places it is said that a bell was stolen by robbers but in their escape by sea the bell fell out of the boat and was lost. G.W.Manby in 1801 wrote of the St David's lost bell, *"so superstitious were the lower class of people for some time, that they often fancied they heard it ring; presaging storms"*. The author considers that a large bell may have been lost around the year 1380 and that it could still be lying on the sea bed in the northern area of Ramsey Sound. Medeival pottery has been discovered on the seabed in the area off Porthstinan and it is quite likely that there are remains of Viking and Roman boats in the waters near St David's.

One of the first shipwrecks in this area, to which the State Papers refer, is a Southampton ship named AMITY. In December 1668, she was carrying a cargo of fruit and wine from the Spanish port of Malaga. They anchored in Ramsey Sound to shelter from a storm, but while they were there the wind altered direction, the ship broke adrift and was driven northwards. Realizing he could not save the ship, the Master and crew abandoned the vessel in two smaller boats and saved themselves by landing on Ramsey Island. The ship drove on to the rocks near St David's Head, where the local people were quick to descend on the ship as it broke apart. Curiously, the local people did not profit greatly from the wine as it was too difficult to carry overland. The casks themselves or the iron hoops on the barrels seem to have been the attraction. It was reported *"the ship fell into the hands of the rude multitude who turned the wines out to carry the casks away"* and *". . . the country people were so barbarous that they staved the wine casks in so much the Master saved not anything considerable, only some fruit"*.

A similar looting incident happened at Newgale in 1690 when

3

the ship RESOLUTION was blown ashore and robbed *"by the more unmerciful people of the neighbourhood"*. Similar habits are recorded half a century later when the 200 ton Dublin ship MARGARET parted from her anchor cables in October 1754 and came ashore under the Druidston cliffs. Her crew attempted to row ashore but all perished. H.M. Customs stationed 30 men to guard the wreck from the *"populace who appeared in good numbers with hatchets and other instruments of destruction"*. Such evidence can be compared with the stories of Gwyr y Bwyelli Bach (Men of the Little Hatchets) at Pembrey, Carmarthenshire during the same era.

The first month of 1749 saw three ships lost near St David's Head. On 18th January, the 90 ton Liverpool snow, ROSE, outward bound for Jamaica was wrecked under the cliffs of Penberry. Captain Sherlock and all his crew were saved. The following week, Lloyds List records that *"a large ship and a snow, names unknown, are lost off St David's Head and all the people are drowned"*. The author has found small eighteenth century pottery pieces in the location of where the ROSE was lost nearly 250 years ago, unfortunately nothing more has been discovered.

A French ship, laden with brandy, wine and general merchandise at Bordeaux, was outward bound to the West Indies when she was attacked by the British privateer LIVERPOOL. The prize crew lost their bearings in the fog when off Skomer and attempted to anchor in St Bride's Bay. During the night the ship was driven

Silver pieces of eight (Pirate money!) found recently on Newgale beach. They may have come from the French ship PRINCE wrecked there in 1757.

4

by a strong southerly to the northern side of the bay where she was deliberately run ashore. A ballad was sung in the district about the wreck and written down nearly a century and a half later. The wreck is sometimes referred to as the BORDEAUX, lost August 10th 1753 but the author considers it to be the PRINCE from Bordeaux which was lost in 1757. A shortened version of the ballad goes like this;

'Twas on the 10th day of August by the new time

A ship out of Bordeaux full laden with wine,

She came to Skomer Island, 'twas by the south main,

The sea it was covered with mist and the rain,

Their decks was washed up and their barrels in sight

Which made the two pilots to wish them goodnight.

They hoisted their long-boat as so got ashore

And there was eight sailors and two Frenchmen more.

But one of their men more gallant and brave

He steered her in steady into old Roger's cave.

When he cut his cable poor voyage he made

And he cast up his cargo agen the green slade.

Then John Thomas, a farmer, a man of great fame

Was born near the Burrows, brought up to the game

He dreamed a dream that was actually true,

He rose the next morning the sands for to view

He dreamed a dream upon his own bed

That the wreck it was covering the whole limpin bed.

Oh! I have been a wreckman all the days of my life

But now I got some to carry home to my wife.

The news then went out about ten o'clock

Punchcastle and Newgale and down they did flock;

Punchcastle and Newgale they had the best share

Of Madame's rich crimson of Madame's French ware"

The PRINCE may have struck the south end of Newgale, as maps show this area to be called Limpet Bed. When sand levels were low a few years ago some coins, a ship's compass and a weight for weighing French coins were found in the centre of Newgale beach.

The Scarborough vessel INCREASE was blown ashore at Druidston beach in January 1791, and the story is told in great detail by the local rector who was an eye witness to some of the events. The INCREASE was returning from St Kitt's in the West Indies with a large cargo of gunpowder and arms belonging to the Government. She was seen in distress off St David's and by the time she came ashore at Druidston a considerable number of people had assembled. *"As they were the lowest order of the community and had toiled so far solely with the hope of plunder, it may well be conceived that they lost no time in boarding the vessel and loading themselves with her contents as soon as she was accessible. They were the more eager in their exertions because they knew that the gentlemen of the county are extremely vigilant upon such occasions, and fly without delay to the relief of the distressed; for the double purpose of rescuing them from the devouring waves, and protecting them from the rapacity of those who are waiting among the rocks to ravish from them the little that the sea has spared. The multitude were in complete possession of their prey. A considerable quantity of the gunpowder was landed from the stranded vessel. Many of the plunderers had loaded themselves with as much as they could carry. Others were struggling for their share of the booty, as their friends threw it from the wreck, by which means much of the powder was scattered on the beach and on the rocks. In this scene of general confusion one of the pillagers in the vessel, either irritated at the eagerness of those on shore, and at the waste which it occasioned, or out of mere unthinking wantoness, swore a dreadful oath, that he would presently give them enough to satisfy them all. He*

5

Dismantling a wrecked ship.

then snatched up a musket and dashed it with great violence against a rock. A single spark was sufficient to produce a most tremendous explosion."

The explosion caught the crowd in a ball of flame. Sixty men and women were caught in the blast and some of them were thrown into the air and killed outright. It brought instant pandamonium, the long skirted women were enveloped in flames and screamed in terror as they were caught in the fire. Everyone who was close to the wreck was burnt. Eight people were killed as a result and others wore the burn marks on their faces for the rest of their lives. Despite the tragedy, the stripping of the stores, rigging and small articles continued until the

militia arrived the following night. Three men were arrested for stealing, but were later acquitted at Haverfordwest Assizes. Although the INCREASE was lost, the Captain, ten man crew and a woman who was on board survived the ordeal. The rector later commented that the fire showed 'Providential Judgement' and added *"may all be warned of such depredations". His words may have been heeded, for, nineteen years later the ship LINEN HALL outward bound for the West Indies came ashore at Nolton Haven. This time it was not robbed and the timbers and rigging were actually sold to the villagers.*

The Government Revenue Cutter PELHAM became involved in a confrontation with smugglers in

6

Porthlysgi in May 1770. The smugglers who were Irish had three vessels, two large cutters and a wherry, (an open boat used by smugglers). The outcome of the skirmish was that they got the better of the Revenue Cutter which they left plundered and wrecked on the south side of Ramsey Island much to the annoyance of the Customs men who were inadequately equipped and totally outnumbered.

The American ship PHEBE & PEGGY, lost at Solva in 1773.

One of the most pitiful wreck stories of West Wales is that of the Philadelphia ship PHEBE & PEGGY which was lost near Solva in 1773. The ship made a fast Atlantic passage from Philadelphia and arrived off the Welsh coast in twenty six days. The first land sighted was Ramsey Island and although they attempted to go north, hurricane force winds complicated by the strong currents drove them towards Solva. Try as they might to sail the ship out of St Bride's Bay, the wind was too strong and by nightfall the vessel had hit the rocks beneath St Elvis and was rapidly breaking apart.

So violent was the storm that the passengers were unable to get into the boats and within a short time all the crew and passengers were struggling for their lives in the water. News of the wreck soon reached the nearby village of Solva and in response four local men immediately manned a rowing boat and set out to perform a rescue. They succeeded in picking up some of the survivors but, on their return to the harbour, disaster struck again. The full fury of the storm was hitting the Black Rock at the harbour mouth and just as the loaded boat entered Solva a breaking wave overtook it. Suddenly the boat was swamped, capsized and all the occupants, the rescued and rescuers alike, were thrown into the boiling surf and drowned. The bodies of three of the local men were later washed ashore, they were Henry John, William Woolcock and Peter Richard. The wreck provided other equally tragic stories. Mrs Elliot, a wealthy passenger, was drowned and her body washed ashore with 500 guineas in her pocket, it is said that old Luke Davy and a John Philip discovered the money and quickly took it, but not being satisfied, broke her fingers to take her rings and split her ears to take her expensive earrings. Mrs Elliot's nephew was one of the few survivors of the sinking but he failed to recover many of her possessions.

Another pitiful event has become a local legend. Amongst the bodies, which came ashore the following day, was that of a drowned mother clutching her dead baby in her arms. These were discovered by a pregnant woman who

7

lived in a humble cottage in the Gwadn Valley close to the beach. The poor woman took the clothes off the dead child in readiness for her own baby. This was not to be, she later died while giving birth to a still-born child. A local ballad of the incident concludes with this message; *"When you rises in the morning, Pray to God to give his blessing - For no one knows at sunrising What may happen before the evening"*.

Lloyds List dated February 8th 1773 records the event, *"PHOEBE & PEGGY, Capt. M'Cullough, from Philadelphia to Newry, on 19 Ult. (19th January 1773) was lost on the rocks in St Brides Bay, near Solva, with the greatest part of the cargo, 3 of her crew, 12 passengers and 4 men who went out to perform a rescue were drowned"*.

A more successful rescue was performed a few years later off Pencarnon. This time it was by a remarkable woman, Mrs Williams of Treleddyn. She, and her husband, were extremely observant of the ships passing up and down the coast and, through her telescope one morning she saw some men stranded on one of the Middle Bishop rocks. Her husband was not there to help, so undaunted she launched a small sailing and rowing boat and succeeded in reaching the seamen. The men were the crew of a Swedish vessel that had sunk nearby and they had managed to get onto the rock where they were stranded, a mile offshore. Imagine their surprise at being rescued by a lone woman. She not only got them safely ashore but fed them until they could return home.

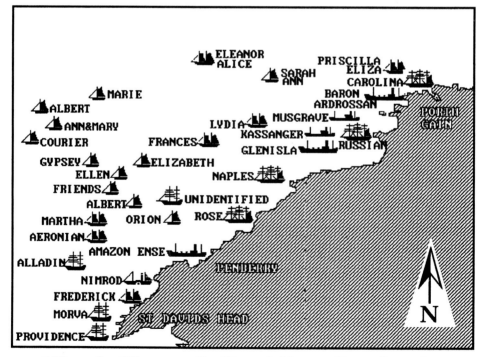

Wreck Chart - St David's to Porthgain

Shipwrecks from 1800 to 1850

The size of this book only permits the author to write about a small number of the shipwrecks that have occurred in this area. We know of more than eighty vessels that have been wrecked in the first half of the nineteenth century, (see wreck list at the end of this book).

January 1802 saw a violent storm in St Brides Bay. The ship DIANA on a voyage from St Croix in the West Indies to Cork was wrecked in the bay and another ship NYMPH smashed up on St Brides Cliff with a huge loss of life, 15 bodies from the ship were buried in the Parish Church graveyard. The sea area to the immediate west of Little Haven known as Goultrop Roads was an anchorage of some importance in the early days of sail. Here vessels could anchor to either shelter from the prevailing winds, to wait for a tide or to collect fresh water. The disadvantage of the anchorage was that if the wind veered to the North or North-east they were trapped with little sea-room in which to sail away. Often they were forced to stay put relying on their anchors, some of which did not hold, causing the vessels to be pounded onto the rocks. Many of the vessels so lost were the smaller sloops and schooners, usually in the coastal trade and often with a Welsh master and crew.

Unlike other areas of the coast, the shipwrecked crews at Goultrop were usually saved and often rescued by local people. One such loss was the sloop HOPE in March 1827. A small sailing vessel of 21 tons, the HOPE was built by John Havard and his son Levi on the banks of the Nevern at Newport, Pembrokeshire in 1805. Carrying a cargo of slates, oats and coal from Pembroke to her home port of Newport, she was driven ashore and wrecked at Goultrop Roads. Her crew was saved. This loss prompted her owners to build their largest vessel, a snow of 182 tons, which was built in 1827 and named HOPE. A snow is similar to a brig rig with square sails on each mast but has an additional trysail mast stepped immediately abaft the mainmast. A similar loss happened in October 1846 when the 21 year old Cardigan schooner BRITON, with a cargo of iron ore from Barrow to Cardiff. The 61 ton schooner had been lying at anchor for two days when she broke away and became a total wreck. Again the crew managed to save themselves. In contrast to the Goultrop area where the crews were usually saved, the area of coast near St David's Head showed no mercy and if ships were driven ashore the seamen had little chance of survival. Exposed to the northerly winds, when the ships drove into the high cliffs it was usual for the entire crew to be lost, together with the vessel and all the cargo.

A ferocious storm in February 1833 caused devastation in the region of St David's Head. No less than 3 vessels were wrecked.

With a cargo of Demerara sugar, intended for Liverpool, the ship CATHERINE of Belfast was wrecked at Porthmelgan and the mate was drowned. The sugar cargo was washed out and very little of the ship was saved. Also with a cargo intended for Liverpool was the Bideford schooner BOLINA. She came ashore on Whitesands beach where her crew were saved and most of the pig iron was also recovered. The third and most tragic loss was the FREDERICK, a schooner outward bound from Liverpool for West Afica. All her crew were drowned when the two masted schooner sank on the north side of St David's Head. Remnants of both the BOLINA and the FREDERICK are still to be seen today. When sand levels are low on the right hand side of Whitesands beach, the oak rib tops of a wreck are discernable jutting up through the sand, this is the BOLINA. In 1970 divers located the site of the FREDERICK after seeing a concreted mass of brown-bess muskets on the seabed, and a subsequent archeological expedition has recovered an anchor, cannon, glass beads, flints, clay pipes and trinkets from the site.

In January 1846 the Pembrokeshire Herald reported an incident when a large brig entered Solva harbour to shelter from a gale. The captain of a French lugger saw the brig and followed her closely into the harbour. When the French captain went ashore he wanted a copy of the local chart. The newspaper commented *"and poor fellow if he had one we really believe that he would never have found his way to Solva as the harbour is so imperfectly marked thereon, which is a great pity considering its capabilities, as many lives together with vessels and valuable*

Early photograph of a hulk lying in Solva Harbour, possibly one of the barques lost in the St Brides Bay (Welsh Industrial & Maritime Museum).

cargoes, thereby might be saved." They were prophetic words for ten months later an unidentified sloop attempted to get into the harbour but ran ashore on the rocks of St Elvis.

The Pembrokeshire Herald dated 20th November 1846 takes up the story . . . *"She had 6 persons on board, five men and one woman. Two of the men, when she struck, got in to the boat, which was immediately capsized and they were drowned. The others (with the exception of the woman, who was tied to the rigging, and also drowned) had gotten upon a small rock which was surrounded by breakers and all efforts to rescue them were unavailing. It is feared that they cannot survive the night. The name of the vessel is unknown. From a letter picked up the name of the Captain is supposed to be Wheelan, from Dungarvan."* The following week there was some criticism that not enough effort was made to save them. One witness, however, provides us with more information. *"At 4.30pm an attempt was made to blow a rope from a small cannon, but it was not the proper one for such work, for the rope was burnt even in the cannon's mouth, as it was not cased in lead or something else that was fireproof. Awful indeed it was! To see four of our fellow creatures naked on a small rock within 100 yards of the shore, and the stormy billows dashing their foam, and pouring out their rage like mountain torrents upon them. They were left to perish."*

The story is related in a slightly different way by writers one hundred years later. They attribute the name VICTORIA to this vessel and say that the vessel washed itself ashore the following morning and with the conjecture that if they had stayed aboard they might have been saved.

From the 1830's to the 1860's there were a considerable number of trading vessels lost in Ramsey Sound, many of them coming or going to the Cardigan Bay ports. Some examples are; the New Quay sloops DOLPHIN lost in 1831, COMMERCE in 1844, ATLANTIC in 1846, the Cardigan sloops MOLLY in 1841, MOLLY LLOYD in 1842, VICTORIA in 1845, and the Tresaith sloop NEW HOPE in 1845. One sloop, typical of the day was the ACTIVE, 26 ton carvel built in Cardigan she was lost, together with her crew, in Ramsey Sound in October 1846 while on a voyage from Swansea to her home port of Cardigan.

Some ships are lost without trace, others can be lost without their names being traced. In boisterous weather in October 1846 a barque was driven on to the cliffs of Abereiddy. There were no survivors and although the ship was thought to be from the Russian port of Archangel, her name was never known. She carried a cargo of pitch, tar and tallow. Two different diving clubs have found brass rudder pintols which are likely to have come from this vessel, perhaps one day her identity will be known.

Built in Salem, Massachusetts in 1833 the barque NAPLES of Boston, was on her way to Dublin in 1849. Her cargo was wheat and maize corn intended for Ireland where they were still suffering from the potato famine. The ship anchored near to the coast but in the night the wind shifted and

The American ship NAPLES being wrecked near Abereiddy in 1849, sketched by one of the survivors. The author managed to locate artefacts from the seabed after seeing this picture in the Ship Inn at Trevine (Ship Inn Trevine).

drove her from her anchors. She struck Carreg Gwylan near Abereiddy and sank nearby. The local people were quick to respond. A small boat was launched from Abereiddy and succeeded in saving 9 crewmen. The Captain, 3 officers and one seaman remained on board, hanging on to the rigging, the only part of the vessel above the waves. The local inhabitants hurried along the cliffs taking with them rescue equipment in the form of a line throwing mortar cannon and a speaking horn. It is unclear from the newspaper if they were successful in saving the remaining 5 people. One report says 9 were saved and 5 were drowned, another report says that all 14 were saved, let us hope that the latter was correct. The author initiated a search for this wreck after seeing a painting of the rescue in the Ship Inn at Trevine. So far copper hull pins, pottery and anchors have been located on the seabed.

Early Steamship Wrecks

The earliest steam driven ships were seen off St David's in the 1830's. These were paddle driven with crude boilers only operating at about 8 pounds per square inch pressure with no gauges. Their engines were unreliable and consequently the ships were fully rigged, to make full use of the wind, and also as a precaution against engine failure. Amongst some of the earlier steam ships lost on the coast of Wales was the ROBERT BRUCE lost off Anglesey in 1820, the FROLIC wrecked on the Nash Sands in March 1831 and the ROTHSAY CASTLE off Beaumaris in August of the same year. The earliest steam packet to be wrecked on the Pembrokeshire coast was the ALBION lost near Jack Sound in 1837.

The first steam driven ship to be lost in the St Davids area was not, as expected, a paddle steamer, but was a screw (propeller) driven vessel in 1855. Owned by the Belfast and London Packet Company the MORNA was bound from Belfast taking army recruits to Cowes and carrying general goods to London.

Under the command of Captain Carter the 363 ton MORNA left Belfast at about midnight on Saturday, February 24th 1855. On board were 93 people, including 55 recruits, outward bound to fight in the Crimea War, the majority being young men with little or no experience of the sea or army discipline, a significant factor in the events that were to follow. A heavy fog shrouded the Irish Sea as they proceeded southward and at times

Captain Carter could not even see the bowsprit of his ship. At about 7pm, just as those on board saw breakers ahead, the ship shuddered to a stop. She had crashed into the North Bishop Rock.

The MORNA wrecked on the North Bishop in 1855.

Many of the young men were experiencing their first sea voyage and in the panic too many of them jumped into a lifeboat before it was out of the davits and it fell apart. Also in the haste to abandon ship another lifeboat was smashed in the swell as it was being lowered. In the end, three quarters survived but 21 people drowned. It was considered that if greater discipline had been enforced when the MORNA was abandoned, there would have been fewer fatalities.

Five years later, under the cliffs of St David's Head, there was a tragedy of even greater proportions. This time the vessel was a paddle steamer owned by the Cork Steamship Company. It was 10pm on the night of February 27th 1860, when Captain Pearn in command of the CITY OF PARIS, a Cork and Milford steamer, sighted the paddle steamer NIMROD

Square sternlight recovered from the wreck of the NIMROD.

George's Channel, and out of sight of land, the engine developed trouble and finally stopped. This was not the first time the 300 horse power engine had caused problems. Some four years before, on the same route, there had been a boiler explosion ripping the engine room apart and killing 6 people. Captain Lyall's decision to decline assistance was a decision he was to regret before the night was over.

During the night the wind increased and bad weather loomed before them. The force of the wind, already a strong westerly, increased to a storm and the already crippled NIMROD could make no headway. Helpless, the disabled paddle steamer with 45 people on board was slowly driven towards the cliffs of St David's Head.

At 8am some residents of St Davids hurried to the headland with the news that a shipwreck was imminent. By the time they arrived it was too late. What they saw was a scene of horror and chaos. The NIMROD had been pounded to bits on the rocks, 100 feet beneath them. There was no way down the cliff and there was nothing any of them could do but watch the pitiful sight of the people drowning before their eyes.

News got back to William Williams, acting Lloyd's agent and Coastguard, who immediately asked if the Manby Rocket apparatus should be taken. The reply was that by the time it could get there the people would already be saved or dead. Mr Williams took a horse and galloped the few miles to the cliff top, what he

about 15 miles off the Smalls Lighthouse. He could see that the NIMROD had her sails set and that her engines had stopped so he investigated and hailed her Captain, Captain Lyall, and enquired if he could be of assistance, to which the reply came *"What will you tow us into Milford for?"*. Captain Pearn said *"£1,000"*, to which Captain Lyall offered £100. *"It is out of the question"* replied Captain Pearn *"but I'll tow you to Milford and leave the remuneration to be settled by the owners"*. This was not accepted by Captain Lyall who then requested that Captain Pearn report the NIMROD's engine failure on his arrival at Waterford.

At the time, the weather was moderate and Captain Lyall, a Scotsman who had been with the Cork Steamship Company for many years, was confident of sailing to Milford without assistance. The NIMROD had left Liverpool at 10am the previous morning with passengers and general cargo for Cork. When, in the middle of St

14

The paddle steamer NIMROD was wrecked at St David's Head in 1860 while taking passengers from Liverpool to Cork. All passengers and crew were drowned.

Sounding Lead recovered from the NIMROD wreck site.

then saw is best described in his own words. *"On my arrival there was not a vestige of the wreck to be seen. The vessel had already parted into three pieces, had gone down in deep water and every soul had perished"*. It was also reported that Captain Lyall was last seen clutching at the stern rail with his head in his hands.

The cargo of general goods, which was irretrievable, was worth £7,000, the Company had insured it for £5,000. The NIMROD herself had undergone a thorough refit only 12 months previously. The Board of Trade inquiry accepted the evidence given to them by those aboard the

CITY OF PARIS. Captain Pearn said that had he for a moment envisaged such an awful calamity, no thought of money would have crossed his mind. Likewise the court considered that Captain Lyall would not have allowed the CITY OF PARIS to leave had he foreseen the slightest danger to his ship, passengers or crew.

The next steamer to be lost was the LLANELLY, built and registered at Llanelli in 1873. She had two engines but only seventy five horse power in total which was insufficient to keep the 141 ton burthen steamer from running aground on the Middle Bishops where she sank.

Sterncarving of the Danish barque CAROLINA, lost at Porthgain in the great gale of 1859 (Sloop Inn, Porthgain).

Shipwrecks from 1850 to 1900

During this period a greater number of vessels were lost than at any other time. This was due to the increase in maritime trade and the consequent increase in vessel movements around the coast. Inevitably human error and also the effects of adverse weather took its toll.

One of the most disastrous storms to hit the Welsh coastline happened in October 1859. Such was the scale of the hurricane that more than 100 vessels were wrecked around Wales during two furious days and nights. The event is sometimes referred to as the 'Royal Charter Gale', for that was the ship lost in Moelfre, Anglesey, that made the headlines when about 450 men, women and children were drowned. There was also severe loss of life in the St David's area. In the forty miles of coastline between Cardigan and St David's Head no less than nine ships were wrecked and a total of 40 lives were lost, an average of one life lost per mile of coast. Some of the ships were lost with their

entire crew, for example the barque CHARLES HOLMES which was lost near Abermawr.

The Danish barque CAROLINA, registered in Copenhagen, was on a voyage from Dublin to Cardiff in ballast. Caught in the storm, her master, Captain Ibsen, skilfully sailed the ship directly into the harbour of Porthgain. His action saved all 13 people on board who climbed ashore over the bowsprit. His ship, however, was a total loss and in coming ashore it destroyed a small wooden pier. A stern carving of this wreck can be seen adorning The Sloop public house in Porthgain.

Crewmen of another much smaller vessel, caught in the same storm were not so lucky. The 24 ton smack ORION of Porthmadoc foundered with her slate cargo somewhere off St David's Head, her 3 crew were lost. Daniel Williams, Master of the schooner MARTHA prudently took shelter and anchored off Pencarnon (one mile to the south of Whitesands) during the first day of the storm. He was taking a cargo of pitwood from

Aberaeron to the schooner's home port of Neath. All went well until the storm increased and turned to the north. All the vessels sheltering from the southerly winds were now caught on a lee shore. The MARTHA's anchors, like so many that night, could not take the strain and the vessel was driven against the rocks. The crew, luckily, saved themselves and the pit props, intended for the South Wales coalfields, became strewn all over the bay.

The Dewsland & Kemes Guardian dated April 13th, 1872 gives the following news: *"On the 27th March as the oyster vessels in the Milford trade were going through Ramsey Sound for the purpose of dredging off Fishguard, one of them called the NEW FASHION of Colchester ran on the rocks known as the Bitches, and was so much damaged that she sank near St David's Head, the crew being saved by the OLD FASHION of Colchester, another of the vessels in the same trade, and taken back to Milford. The lost vessel was a new one and the fastest sailor in the fleet".*

The next loss near St David's Head was an extremely elderly vessel. The sloop ANN & MARY, lost in April 1873, was unusual in that she was 111

Not a shipwreck but a tranquil scene of the steamer ENDCLIFFE beached at Porthmelgan in September 1914. (Dr G. W. Middleton)

years old when lost. Built in Newport, Pembrokeshire, in 1762 and of only 15 tons, her builders and owners must have taken special care of her as the average lifetime of similar local vessels was about 30 years.

In 1876 the Aberayron Steam Navigation Company lost their 12 year old screw steamer PRINCE CADWGAN on Carreg Fran near Porthclais. The steamer was of 111 tons and clinker built on iron frames in Lanarkshire in 1864. The PRINCE CADWGAN was returning from Bristol to Aberaeron with petroleum fuel, when her propeller was knocked off on a submerged rock. The steamer drove ashore but all the crew escaped onto the rocks. The following day, the Captain returned across the rocks to the wreckage. He got to Carreg Fran but was cut off by the tide and could not return until the next low water.

A 4 year old Whitehaven tug was the next steamer wrecked in the area in 1879. The 85 ton WHITEHAVEN was steaming southward through Ramsey Sound when she hit the notorious Horse Rock, an unseen hazard that lurks beneath the swirling waters of the Sound. It is an underwater obstruction that has caused scores of wrecks. Careless navigation on the part of her Master was blamed for the loss of the tug, that sank in deep water, all hands were saved.

The next steamer casualty was also a tug, the Liverpool registered BRITISH KING, that hit Shoe Rock in April 1881 and sank. The ten man crew was saved. The wreck was

purchased by a Milford salvor who put two barges above the wreck and carried out a tidal lift using chains to lift the BRITISH KING. The first two attempts failed when timbers on the barges snapped under the strain. On the third attempt using two tugs they beached the wreck at Porthlysgi. However after their hard work an October gale then sank the two salvage tugs in Porthlysgi. One of these may be the ST GEORGE, well known to local divers.

The Liverpool steamer AMAZON ENSE was wrecked in 1881, this is the ship's wheel boss bearing her name and date of construction.

The Liverpool steamer AMAZON ENSE commenced her final voyage on Friday, April 15th 1881, leaving Liverpool, bound for Le Havre and then on to Lisbon and Para, Brazil. Her Master, Captain Hallgate, was confronted with a thick fog in St George's Channel, nevertheless he proceeded south relying entirely on the steering compass. The first indication that he was not on course was an almighty thud as the steamer hit the headland near St David's Head. So sudden was the shock that one crew member died of fright. The steamer, built two years before in Southampton, rapidly filled with water and she sank in shallow water, leaving the bow above the waves, the stern underwater, and five metres of water in the holds. The hull was so badly damaged that refloating was out of the question and the wreck was sold by auction, where she lay, a few weeks later.

There was an inquiry at her home port of liverpool in May 1881 and some criticism was made of Captain Hallgate who had his certificate suspended for three months. The court deemed that the AMAZON ENSE was travelling at '*too high a rate of speed*', in other words, far too fast, considering the foggy conditions. The AMAZON ENSE was an iron ship and her compasses had not been corrected for the trip.

A paddle tug was purposely driven onto the sand at Whitesands Beach in order to save the vessel and those on board after it had hit Horse Rock. The remains can still be seen today at low water at the south end of the beach. Her name is the GUIDING STAR, a Liverpool paddle tug, wrecked in May 1885.

In February 1886, Captain Wallace was helming his Glasgow steamer, GLENISLA, southward with a full cargo of coal to the Mediterranean port of Savona when he made a navigational error. He saw the light of the South Bishop Lighthouse but mistook it for a light on the Irish coast and altered course, hitting the

Detail of a silver fork handle showing the name GLENISLA. This helped confirm the wreck site of the steamer lost on Abereiddy reefs in 1886.

underwater reefs off Abereiddy. Fortunately all on board, including his wife, were saved by launching the ship's boats and rowing ashore.

In December 1890 a small 65 foot long steamer named MAGGIE ANN carrying stone from Porthgain, intended for making roads in Southampton, sank near Abereiddy. This is one steamer that divers have not yet located.

19

Shipbuilder's brass plate from the COUNT D'ASPREMONT.

With full sails set the barque SUZANNE BOULET, of Rouen, smashed into the southern part of Ramsey Island in March 1891. Her bows hit the cliffs and she immediately went over on her beam ends. Fortunately, all the French crew landed safely on the island. An anchor of this sailing ship was recovered and is now to be seen outside the Royal George in Solva.

The following year the Newcastle steamer MUSGRAVE, together with her cargo of coal, was lost on one of the Abereiddy reefs. She hit the reef in a November fog and the 10 crewmen rowed themselves ashore to Abereiddy where they stayed the night in three of the cottages. Returning to their lifeboats the next morning they found that what few possessions they had saved had been stolen.

The LEWIS, a Beaumaris schooner was taking a cargo of Porthmadoc slates to Folkestone in 1894, when her mainsail broke, off the North Bishops. Intending to sail to Milford for repairs, the schooner developed a leak and sank in the water south of Ramsey Sound, the crew escaping in the ship's boat before their vessel sank beneath the waves. Part of the cargo of slates has now been recovered and has been used to reroof the terraced cottages at Porthgain.

An Irish steamer taking a cargo of coal from Newport, Gwent to Belfast was the next victim of Horse Rock in Ramsey Sound. The ship's bell of this small steamer, ROSTREVOR, lost in 1898, was found by divers in 1981.

Shipwrecks Since 1900

The bulk of the maritime losses occurred in the latter half of the nineteenth century, however, vessels have regularly come to grief on the rocks surrounding St David's throughout the twentieth century.

In 1903, the large steamer GRAFFOE hit the rocks at the southern entrance to Ramsey Sound. 14 Men escaped in one of the ship's lifeboats and were later rescued, but there were others on board who were not so lucky. The ship sank in shallow water leaving only her masts above the waves and during the night the Chief Engineer and Captain were both washed away. Nobody on shore noticed the desperate plight of the 7 survivors who were stuck in the rigging waiting for rescue for over a day in a January gale. They had to endure a further night before the lifeboat came to rescue them, in the meantime, one man died from hypothermia.

Later in the same year the Shipping Gazette reported as follows:
"St Davids, December 9th, 6 pm, Steamer COUNT D'ASPREMONT of Swansea, Captain Wood, from Dublin for Newport in ballast; fast ashore on Horse Rock, Ramsey Sound, likely to become a total wreck. Crew saved in their own boat". The ship eventually sank some distance north of the rock and her upturned hull was discovered by diver friends of the author in 1982.

One of the largest steamers to be lost in the region was the Houlder line LANGTON GRANGE that struck Bell Rock in a fog in 1909. This incident was responsible for the Admiralty considering different

The steamer GRAFFOE hit the cliffs of Ynys Bery and sank in January 1903. Her crew were forced to survive for 48 hours frozen in the rigging before being rescued, 3 men lost their lives.

A sketch from the author's dive notes after visiting the wreck of the COUNT D'ASPREMONT lying upside down on the seabed of Ramsey Sound.

hazard markings on charts. One month later another steamer was to be lost on the south side of Ramsey Island. With a cargo of flour intended for Glasgow, the Croatian steamer SZENT ISTVAN ran straight into the cliffs to the west of Porth Llauog. Fortunately, the crews of both steamers were saved. The wreck of the SZENT ISTVAN was half afloat for about a week and the cargo of flour washed out onto the beaches. The inhabitants of St David's and Solva were soon collecting up the flour off the beaches in all sorts of containers, including pillowcases. The local newspaper commented that the churches were only half full that Sunday because people were more interested in collecting flour than attending Church.

The next disaster was the St David's Lifeboat itself. It was lost together with 3 men while going to the rescue of a ketch in 1910, (see next chapter).

In 1915 a November gale caused the loss of two large sailing ships on the North Pembrokeshire Coast. One was the CALBURGA, a barque carrying timber from Halifax, Nova Scotia, which was lost near Strumble Head and the other was the Norwegian barque FORMOSA also carrying Canadian timber. The FORMOSA was abandoned by her crew when near the Middle Bishops, all the men were saved, 11 by the St David's Lifeboat and others came ashore in their own boat at Whitesands. The barque did not sink, as expected, and was taken in tow to a beach near Milford Haven where her hull was set alight by vandals.

The Cardiff cargo steamer CYMRIC PRINCE was wrecked on Bell Rock in February 1917. She was on a voyage from Mellila to West Hartlepool with a cargo of iron ore. Her remains now lie intermingled with those of the LANGTON GRANGE.

22

The steamer EMMANUEL became stranded in Ramsey Sound in 1925. Although she was got off, she was considered a total constructive loss and was scrapped. In the background can be seen the Lifeboathouse at St Justinian. (Welsh Industrial and Maritime Museum 83.605).

23

Three months later the Liverpool steamer COLONIAN carrying a general cargo from Boston, Massachusetts to London sank at the southern end of the North Bishop Rock. All 47 on board were saved.

A Greek steamship EMMANUEL grounded on the rocks in Ramsey Sound in March 1925 *(see photograph)*. All the men climbed ashore aswell as numerous black rats. The damaged hull was stopped up with cement which lasted long enough for the ship to be floated and taken to Milford Haven. The damage was found to be too severe and she was eventually broken up.

The PORTLAND, an aged 54 ton auxiliary sailing vessel, carrying a cargo of stone gravel from Porthgain to Pembroke, sank in Porthlysgi in December 1927. Two years later a dense fog caused the Dutch trawler GARAD to be lost on the west side of Ramsey Island at Carreg Gwylan.

There were a few Second World War losses in the region but the most curious sinking in the 1940's was the mysterious loss of the ALBANY (ex EMPIRE ALBANY) in November 1946. With a cargo of 250 tons of coal from Port Talbot to Rosslare this steamer never arrived and her fate and that of her entire crew was never ascertained. The steamer never cleared the Pembrokeshire Coast and the first indication of her loss was when bodies and a lifeboat washed ashore at Caerfai, another empty lifeboat came ashore at Whitesands but none of the crew was ever seen alive again. It is possible that the ship hit a rogue mine and quickly sank somewhere in St Bride's Bay.

In the summer of 1979 two Frenchmen in the 24 foot yacht LOTUS were caught out in a severe hurricane off the Smalls. The older man was washed away and in desperation, the other man, who had little sailing ability sailed the yacht directly onto Newgale Beach, saving both himself and the yacht. The body of his lost companion was picked up by the Fishguard Ferry one week later.

A most remarkable set of events caused the last notable losses in this region. It happened in 1981 when the Greek Vernicos Company was taking three ex Mersey Tugs to Piraeus. One tug was towing the other two, when the towing tug developed engine trouble. They stopped to deal with the problem and then recommenced the tow, only to find that the towrope (800 meters long) had fouled the propeller of the towing tug. Divers went out in a fast inflatable from Solva to help but failed to find the tugs because they had been given incorrect bearings. In the meantime, poor weather had driven all three tugs into the rocks. A combined operation of the Brawdy Sea King Helicopter and the St David's Lifeboat took all the men off but all three tugs became stranded under Solva cliffs. It was an unusual scenario of three identical vessels being lost in the same place at the same time. Within a few years the destructive power of the waves caused the wreckage of all three tugs to be pounded into the rocks. (See photograph on the back cover).

The motor vessel RUM RUNNER lying stranded on the notorious Horse Rock in the middle of Ramsey Sound in 1932. (Malcolm James Collection).

Lifeboats & Lifeboatmen

The area of Goultrop, to the south of Little Haven had an early rowing and sailing Lifeboat at the end of the nineteenth century and the remnants of the Lifeboat house can still be seen at the foot of the cliffs. Little Haven now has an Inshore Lifeboat which does valuable service to small craft in need of rescue in St Brides Bay.

The St David's Lifeboat was established in 1869 at the request of the local inhabitants. The first lifeboat, named AUGUSTA, was a 32 foot rowing lifeboat using ten Oarsmen, a Bowman, a Second Cox and the Coxwain. The AUGUSTA Lifeboat was launched 17 times between 1869 and 1885 and saved 23 lives, her Coxwain was David Hicks, who served as Coxwain for 23 years. The most meritous rescue being to save 9 sailors from the wreck of the MYSTIC TIE in 1877.

In 1885, a new 12 oared rowing and sailing Lifeboat, the GEM, came to the Lifeboat house at St Justinian. She was launched 19 times and saved 16 lives including a dramatic rescue from the steamer GRAFFOE in 1903.

The greatest tragedy to befall any of the West Wales Lifeboat Stations happened on 13th October 1910, when the St David's Lifeboat together with three of her lifeboatmen, including the Coxwain, were lost while performing a rescue.

St David's Lifeboat GEM being launched at St Justinian. This sailing and rowing lifeboat was wrecked on the Bitches in 1910 and 3 Lifeboatmen were lost. (RNLI)

A North easterly gale was blowing down Ramsey Sound on the night of 12th October and the Master of the ketch DEMOCRAT, fearing that the ketch's two anchors would not hold her, sent signals of distress to the Lifeboat Station. The Lifeboat GEM was launched into the heavy seas of the Sound and after two unsuccessful attempts came alongside the ketch that was riding at anchor just north of the dangerous reef known as "The Bitches".

Photograph of the St David's Lifeboat taken about 1914. Unless a reserve Lifeboat, this will be the GENERAL FARRELL. (Dr G.W. Middleton).

The 3 man crew of the DEMOCRAT jumped into the Lifeboat and orders were given to sheer off. What happened next is best described by the Lifeboat Journal (February 1st, 1911). *"Although the crew pulled hard they were unable to straighten the Lifeboat's head up against the wind, sea and tide, and she rapidly swept towards the reef. Seeing that it was impossible to pull clear the Coxwain made an effort to manoeuvre his boat through a narrow passage, which in the darkness was only discernable by its foam, the sea in the whole vicinity being described as "boiling mad". Unfortuni.:ely, in attempting to make this passage the Lifeboat struck on a rock, and all the men were thrown out, some on to the rock and some into the sea, the Lifeboat being washed away and totally wrecked.*

15 men including the crew of the DEMOCRAT, succeeded in getting upon the rock, but John Stephens, the Coxwain, and two other Lifeboatmen were not seen again until their bodies were picked up. On land nothing was known of the accident until about 9am when one of the men on the rock burnt some oilskins to attract attention".

Sidney Mortimer, and two Coastguards set out from Porthclais in an open 20 foot boat. A heavy squall caught them when they reached the Sound which broke their rigging and nearly swamped them. They could see the survivors clinging to the rocks but as the tide was against them they waited four hours for the tide to fall. Eventually they took 5 men off the rock and landed them on Ramsey Island. Returning, they took 5 more ashore, and were going back a third time when another boat rescued the remaining men. The Fishguard Lifeboat CHARTERHOUSE, one of the first motorised RNLI Lifeboats, arrived on the scene but was too late to help with the rescue.

The Greek owned oil tanker WORLD CONCORD broke in two in a hurricane in 1954. In an outstanding rescue the St David's Lifeboat saved all the men on the aft section.

In 1911 a new motorised Lifeboat, GENERAL FARRELL, came to St Justinian and it was at this time when the Lifeboat House and slipway was constructed above the original slipway. In 1936 a new lifeboat SWN Y MOR arrived and was to be responsible for saving no less than 108 lives, mainly through the years of World War Two.

A tempest in St George's Channel in November 1954 caused a Liberian flagged oil tanker the WORLD CONCORD to break in half. 7 men including the Master found themselves on the forepart and 35 crewmen were on the stern section. The St David's Lifeboat, in tremendous seas, rescued the men from the sternpart and the Rosslare

Lifeboat rescued the others. The two halves of the oil tanker were put together again and one year later the ship was sailing the seas again.

A further tragedy was to befall St David's when lifeboatman Ieuan Bateman was washed out of the Lifeboat and drowned when it was returning from a service rescue in 1956.

In 1963 this Lifeboat was replaced with the JOSEPH SOAR, a Watson type, that rescued 27 lives, including 3 from the Solva tugs incident, before being replaced in 1986 by the RUBY AND ARTHUR REED. In 1988, St David's had a new Tyne class boat named GARSIDE.

Wreck List

In chronological order this list of shipwrecks covers the area of St Brides Bay, Ramsey Sound, Ramsey Island, The Bishops, St David's Head and Porthgain.

Abbreviations are used to denote ship types;
SS - Steamship, MV - Motor Vessel, TUG - Tug, FRS - Full Rigged Ship, BQ - Barque, BG - Brig, BGN - Brigantine, S - Sailing Ship, SL - Sloop, SM - Smack, K - Ketch, LB - Lifeboat, CUT - Sailing Cutter.

Ship Name	Lost	Type	Location
AMITY	1668/12	S	ST DAVIDS HEAD
RESOLUTION	1669/09/01	FRS	NEWGALE
ALICE & BARBARA	1747	S	ST BRIDES BAY
BATCHELOR	1748/01/31	S	ST BRIDES BAY
ROSE	1749/01/17	BGN	PENBERRY
PRINCE	1757/08/10	FRS	NEWGALE
TRITON	1763	BG	LITTLE HAVEN
PELHAM	1770/05/02	CUT	RAMSEY ISLAND
PHEBE & PEGGY	1773/01/19	FRS	SOLVA
LOOE	1774/08/26	S	ST BRIDES BAY
INCREASE	1791/01	BG	DRUIDSTON
MORVA	1793/11/22	S	ST DAVIDS HEAD
JOHN & MICHAEL	1794/12/12	S	SOLVA
ROSE	1795/12/01	FRS	ST BRIDES BAY
PROVIDENCE	1797/01/31	FRS	ST BRIDES BAY
NYMPH	1802/01	FRS	ST BRIDES
DIANA	1802/01/21	BG	ST BRIDES BAY
VOLUNTEER	1807/04	BG	RAMSEY SOUND
FIDELITY	1807/12/08	S	WHITESANDS
UNION	1809/02/18	FRS	BROADHAVEN
LADY MANSFIELD	1810-1840	S	PENBERRY
LINEN HALL	1810/12/24	S	NOLTON HAVEN
FORTITUDE	1812	BG	SOLVA
WARREN	1815/12/19	S	RAMSEY SOUND
FRIENDS	1819	S	RAMSEY SOUND
BRITANNIA	1822/08/13	S	LITTLE HAVEN
COSSACK	1823/12	S	NEWGALE
ANNE	1825-1860	SL	WHITEANDS
HOPE	1827/03/05	SL	GOULTROP
SUSANNAH	1828/03/13	SL	PORTHLYSGI
THREE SISTERS	1829	SL	ST DAVIDS HEAD
DILIGENCE	1829/07/04	SM	ST BRIDES BAY
DOLPHIN	1831/07/31	SL	RAMSEY SOUND
BOLINA	1833/02/21	SC	WHITESANDS
FREDERICK	1833/02/21	SC	ST DAVIDS HEAD

Ship Name	Lost	Type	Location
CATHERINE	1833/02/21	SC	PORTHMELGAN
EAGLE	1833/03	SL	ST BRIDES BAY
JANE	1833/08/31	SL	ST BRIDES BAY
VENUS	1833/11/29	S	ST BRIDES BAY
EAGLE	1834/03/22	SM	ST BRIDES BAY
CARDIGAN SLOOP	1835/10/08	SL	ST BRIDES BAY
DOGSTAR	1835/10/08	SM	ST BRIDES BAY
CARDIFF BRIG	1838	BG	BISHOPS
HANNAH	1840-1860	SC	ABEREIDDY REEFS
ANN	1840/01/22	BG	NEWGALE
KITTY	1840/02/05	S	RAMSEY SOUND
ALICIA	1841/01/29	SL	ST BRIDES BAY
MOLLY	1841/06/12	SL	RAMSEY SOUND
PERSEVERENCE	1841/12/03	SL	ST BRIDES BAY
JOHN & MARIANNE	1841/12/12	SL	SOLVA
MOLLY LLOYD	1842/09/15	SL	RAMSEY SOUND
COMMERCE	1844/08/06	SL	RAMSEY SOUND
VICTORIA	1845/02/09	SC	SOLVA
PILGRIM	1845/09/23	SL	ST BRIDES BAY
NEW HOPE	1845/10/09	SL	RAMSEY SOUND
AURORA	1846/06/20	SL	NORTH BISHOPS
RUSSIAN BARQUE	1846/10/16	BQ	ABERIEDDY HEAD
BRITON	1846/10/21	SC	GOULTROP ROADS
ACTIVE	1846/10/31	SL	RAMSEY SOUND
VICTORIA	1846/11/20	SC	SOLVA
ATLANTIC	1847/03	SL	PORTHMELGAN
HOPE	1847/12	S	NORTH BISHOP
ELIZABETH MARIA	1848/11	SL	ST BRIDES BAY
PETITE SELINAX	1848/11	S	ST BRIDES BAY
NAPLES	1849/01/25	BQ	ABEREIDDY
LYDIA	1849/11/04	SC	ABEREIDDY REEFS
BEATRICE	1850-1880	SC	SOUTH BISHOPS
ANNIE	1850-1860	S	NEWGALE
JOHN GUISE	1850/06/04	BGN	ABEREIDDY REEFS
ALLADIN	1850/11/05	BG	WHITESANDS

Ship Name	Lost	Type	Location
TERESSA	1851/03/17	SL	ST BRIDES BAY
RUBY	1851/06/09	SL	SOUTH BISHOP
UNIDENTIFIED	1851/09/26	SC	SOUTH BISHOP
ELIZABETH	1852	SC	ST DAVIDS
FERONIA	1852/01/01	SL	ST BRIDES BAY
UNITY	1852/09/18	SL	ST BRIDES BAY
FLORA	1852/11	S	ST DAVIDS
MARY	1853/07/16	S	ST BRIDES BAY
DAPHNE	1854/06/20	SC	ST DAVIDS, OFF
MORNA	1855/02/25	PS	NORTH BISHOP
CONCORDIA	1856	SC	ST BRIDES BAY
AERONIAN	1856/10/21	SC	ST DAVIDS HEAD
RESPIGADERA	1858/09/17	BQ	MIDDLE BISHOPS
DUKE OF WELLINGTON	1859/03/16	SL	RAMSEY SOUND
MARTHA	1859/10/25	SC	ST DAVIDS HEAD
TRUE BESS	1859/10/25	SL	GOULTROP
ORION	1859/10/26	SM	ST DAVIDS HEAD
CAROLINA	1859/10/26	BQ	PORTHGAIN
NIMROD	1860/02/28	PS	ST DAVIDS HEAD
TIVY LASS	1860/08/06	SL	ST BRIDES BAY
ELLEN	1860/08/28	SL	RAMSEY SOUND
AILSA	1861/02/21	BQ	ST BRIDES BAY
ALBERT	1861/04/03	SM	ST DAVIDS HEAD
RACHABITE	1861/09/04	SM	RAMSEY SOUND
LESMAHAGAN	1861/11/30	BQ	SOLVA
OAK	1862	S	SOLVA
LILY	1862/01/05	SL	NEWGALE
EUPHEMIE KERNORVANT	1862/01/24	S	ST BRIDES BAY
GYPSEY	1862/09/25	SM	ST DAVIDS HEAD
FRANCES	1863/05/28	SL	ST DAVIDS HEAD
EUGENIE	1864/07/04	SC	ST BRIDES BAY
CORDELIA	1865/01/16	SC	ST BRIDES BAY
OSPREY	1865/06/10	SL	RAMSEY SOUND
FRIENDS	1865/10/23	SM	ST DAVIDS HEAD
ELLEN	1866/09/11	SM	ST BRIDES BAY
FRANCIS	1867/01/05	SM	RAMSEY SOUND
GOOD HOPE	1867/10/26	SL	RAMSEY SOUND
PRISCILLA ELIZA	1869/07/13	SC	PORTHGAIN
JANE & CATHERINE	1869/09/12	SL	RAMSEY SOUND
AID	1869/09/13	SL	RAMSEY
HOPEWELL	1870/09/30	SL	RAMSEY ISLAND
RESOLUTION	1870/09/30	BG	RAMSEY SOUND
WASP	1870/10/12	SL	GOULTROP
TRANSIT	1870/10/12	SM	RAMSEY SOUND
PRIMA	1870/11	SM	RAMSEY SOUND
ANNE DAVIES	1870/11	S	RAMSEY SOUND
CHESTER	1870/11/22	SM	RAMSEY, OFF
TWO BROTHERS	1872/03	SM	RAMSEY, OFF
NEW FASHION	1872/03/27	SC	ST DAVIDS, OFF
MERSEY	1872/06/05	S	SOUTH BISHOP
LYLY DALE	1872/11	SC	RAMSEY, OFF
OCEAN MONARCH	1872/12/08	SC	GOULTROP
ROSINA	1873/02/03	SC	GOULTROP
PEARL	1873/03/03	SC	GOULTROP
ANN & MARY	1873/04/25	SL	ST DAVIDS, OFF
LLANELLY	1873/05/11	SS	MIDDLE BISHOPS
ELEANOR ALICE	1873/07/21	S	PORTHGAIN, OFF
FAIRY QUEEN	1873/10/10	SM	LITTLE HAVEN
SARAH	1873/10/23	SC	ST BRIDES BAY
ALARIC	1874	S	ST BRIDES BAY
AMITY	1875/01/01	SL	RAMSEY SOUND
TURTLE DOVE	1875/05/06	SL	RAMSEY SOUND
SYLPH	1875/11/14	SC	GOULTROP
ANTELOPE	1875/11/25	CUT	ST BRIDES BAY
CATHERINE	1876/01/04	SM	PORTHCLAIS
ALBACORE	1876/09/23	BGN	LITTLE HAVEN
PRINCE CADWGAN	1876/09/30	SS	CARREG FRAN
MYSTIC TIE	1877/11/11	BGN	RAMSEY ISLAND
ALICE	1878/03/23	SM	LITTLE HAVEN
WHITEHAVEN	1879/05/21	TUG	RAMSEY SOUND
EAGLE	1879/07/29	SS	BISHOPS, OFF
MESSENGER	1879/10/05	BGN	RAMSEY, OFF
COURIER	1879/10/19	SM	PORTHCLAIS
MARIE	1880/04/19	S	ST BRIDES BAY
ANN DAVIES	1880/08/09	SL	ST BRIDES BAY
ALERT	1881/02/03	SM	ST DAVIDS HEAD
BRITISH KING	1881/04/02	SS	RAMSEY SOUND
AMAZON ENSE	1881/04/16	SS	ST DAVIDS HEAD
BRITANNIA	1881/08/19	SM	ST DAVIDS HEAD
ST GEORGE	1881/10/15	PS	PORTHLYSGI
GWEN	1882/04/21	SC	RAMSEY SOUND
ELIZABETH	1882/11/24	SC	RAMSEY ISLAND
STORJOHANN	1882/12	BQ	RAMSEY ISLAND
DAVID	1882/12/16	SM	RAMSEY SOUND

Ship Name	Lost	Type	Location
SOLFERINO	1883/01/25	SC	ST BRIDES BAY
SAINT HELEN	1883/03/01	BGN	BISHOPS, OFF
TAUNTON PACKET	1883/03/02	SC	BISHOPS, OFF
GUIDING STAR	1885/05/19	TUG	WHITESANDS
GLENISLA	1886/02/28	SS	ABEREIDDY REEFS
ROSEOLA	1886/10/15	SL	ST BRIDES BAY
ANN PRITCHARD	1887/04/10	SL	ST DAVIDS, OFF
JOHN WILLIAMS	1887/12/17	SC	LITTLE HAVEN
HENRY JUKE	1890/03/21	S	RAMSEY SOUND
CLYDESDALE	1890/03/28	BQ	SOUTH BISHOP
SUZANNE BOULET	1891/03/03	SL	RAMSEY ISLAND
LIZZIE ANNIE	1891/08/22	K	RAMSEY SOUND
GWENDOLINE	1891/09/16	SS	ST BRIDES BAY
SILOAM	1892/02/22	SS	ST BRIDES BAY
MUSGRAVE	1892/11/25	SS	ABEREIDDY REEFS
MARTHA JANE	1894/03/19	SL	RAMSEY SOUND
LEWIS	1894/03/23	SC	ST BRIDES BAY
OGMORE	1894/04/10	SS	ST BRIDES BAY
SUNLIGHT	1894/04/29	SS	BISHOPS, OFF
UNIDENTIFIED	1895/11/19	S	NORTH BISHOP
CORCYRA	1897/02/10	SS	RAMSEY SOUND
BARON ARDROSSAN	1898/08/21	SS	PORTHGAIN
AGNES FRASER	1898/09/23	SC	WHITESANDS BAY
ROSTREVOR	1898/12/09	SS	RAMSEY SOUND
CLARA FELICIA	1899/09	S	NORTH BISHOP
CASHIER	1900/02/16	BQ	ST BRIDES BAY
RESULT	1902/08/20	K	SOLVA
PECHERIES FR 17	1902/08/22	K	RAMSEY SOUND
DREADNOUGHT	1902/12/04	SC	ST BRIDES BAY
GRAFFOE	1903/01/10	SS	RAMSEY SOUND
COUNT D' ASPREMONT	1903/12/09	SS	RAMSEY SOUND
EDITH CROSSFIELD	1904/05	BQ	NORTH BISHOP
PERCY BATRAM	1906-1909	SC	TRAETHLLYFN
CHRISTINE	1906/11/14	K	SOLVA
ROSS	1906/11/14	SS	BISHOPS, OFF
LANGTON GRANGE	1909/08/05	SS	NORTH BISHOP
SARAH ANN	1909/09/12	SM	PORTHGAIN

Ship Name	Lost	Type	Location
SZENT ISTVAN	1909/09/28	SS	RAMSEY ISLAND
DEMOCRAT	1910/10/12	K	RAMSEY SOUND
GEM	1910/10/13	LB	RAMSEY SOUND
JAMES SHEARER	1913/03/13	SC	ST BRIDES BAY
ALPHA	1914/08/23	K	PORTHGAIN, OFF
FORMOSA	1915/11/12	BQ	RAMSEY, OFF
CYMRIC PRINCE	1917/02/23	SS	NORTH BISHOP
COLONIAN	1917/05/20	SS	NORTH BISHOP
PRIDE OF WALES	1917/11/06	K	NEWGALE
KASSANGER	1918/03/20	SS	ABERIEDDY REEFS
ELIZABETH ALICE	1920/10/07	MV	ST BRIDES BAY
FRENCH SCHOONER	1925	SC	NOLTON HAVEN
EMMANUEL	1925/03	SS	RAMSEY SOUND
PORTLAND	1927/12/09	SC	PORTHLYSGI
GARAD	1929/06/12	MFV	RAMSEY ISLAND
RUM RUNNER	1932/08	MV	RAMSEY SOUND
ENGLISHMAN	1933/05/02	SC	ST BRIDES BAY
UNIDENTIFIED	1936/01/05	SC	MUSSELWICK
HEMATITE	1936/01/05	SS	MIDDLE BISHOPS
CHASMOOR	1936/05/06	SS	BISHOPS
IDA	1940/02/26	MV	ST DAVIDS, OFF
PORT TOWNSVILLE	1941/03/03	MV	ST DAVIDS, OFF
PINK ROSE	1941/05/04	SS	BISHOPS, OFF
BEGERIN	1941/05/18	MV	ST DAVIDS, OFF
NORFOLK COAST	1945/02/28	MV	ST DAVIDS, OFF
KING EDGAR	1945/03/02	MV	BISHOPS, 4M WEST
ALBANY	1946/11/21	SS	ST DAVIDS, OFF
WIEMA	1961/12/10	MV	RAMSEY, OFF
TENET	1970/01/09	MV	MIDDLE BISHOPS
STELLA MARIS	1970/10/13	MFV	PORTHCLAIS
ATTACKER	1974/12/19	MV	NEWGALE
LOTUS	1979/08/20	SL	NEWGALE
FAIRWEATHER	1981/10/20	MFV	RAMSEY SOUND
VERNICOS ALEXIA	1981/10/28	TUG	SOLVA
VERNICOS BARBARA	1981/10/28	TUG	SOLVA
VERNICOS GEORGOS	1981/10/28	TUG	SOLVA
JOHN DOE	1993/12/08	MFV	RAMSEY SOUND

Book List

DEADLY PERILS Peter Davies, Merrivale 1992
PEMBROKESHIRE SHIPWRECKS Ted Goddard, Hughes 1984
SHIPWRECKS AROUND WALES VOL 1 & 2 Tom Bennett, Happy Fish 1992
ST DAVID'S AND DEWISLAND David James, Cardiff 1981
THE STORY OF THE ST DAVID'S LIFEBOAT Desmond Hampson & George
Middleton, St David's 1974

For those interested in researching more about Pembrokeshire's maritime history, the Pembrokeshire Records Office has a list of local registered vessels and early local newspapers. The reference library in Haverfordwest has Pembrokeshire Herald newspapers on microfilm. Newspapers can also be viewed at the National Library of Wales, Aberystwyth or at the British Library Newspaper Library in Colindale.

By the same author:

FISHGUARD LIFEBOATS *(For RNLI funds, 1984)*
SHIPWRECKS AROUND WALES Volume 1 *(1987 & Reprint 1992)*
SHIPWRECKS AROUND WALES Volume 2 *(1992)*

Acknowledgements

I would like to thank all those who have helped in compiling this book. Thanks to my wife Maureen for proofreading and to Sarah Stanbury for the layout and typesetting. I am grateful to Dr George Middleton for providing photographs and to the Welsh Industrial and Maritime Museum and Malcolm James for permission to reproduce photographs. A special thanks must also go to my diving pals, Greg Evans, Jim Phillips, Clive and Cindy of Diving into Adventure, St David's.